The Penitentes

by MARTA WEIGLE

with etchings by Eli Levin

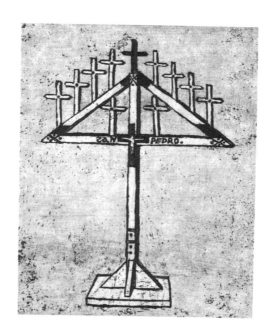

Ancient City Press

P.O. BOX 5401   SANTA FE, NEW MEXICO 87502

International Standard Book Number
0-941270-00-9
Library of Congress Catalog Number
78-131971

10 9 8 7 6

PREFACE

The following essay is a summary presentation of two years' research into published and unpublished sources on the Penitentes of the Southwest. A fully-documented book organizing all this material (some six hundred references) is in process. Hopefully, the projected volume will become an obituary for secondary and sensationalized studies of the Brotherhood. In the meantime, this pamphlet may serve as a brief introduction to Penitente beliefs, practices, organization, and history — insofar as they are known and reported.

A number of people have been most helpful throughout this study. Full acknowledgements will be made in the main work. At this point, I would like to thank Dr. Myra Ellen Jenkins, historian and Deputy for Archives of the New Mexico State Record Center and Archives, for reading and commenting on the text and for making accessible private and especially useful references.

M. W.
Santa Fe
July 3, 1970

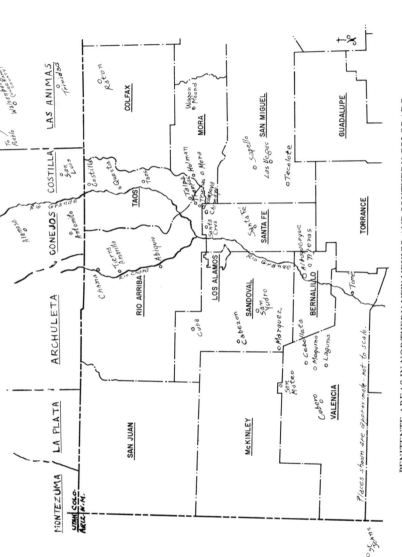

PENITENTE AREAS IN NORTHERN NEW MEXICO AND SOUTHERN COLORADO

Map shows county names and some villages and cities formerly or presently associated with the Penitentes.

INTRODUCTION

The Penitente Brotherhood is a lay religious organization related to the Roman Catholic Church in the southwestern United States, primarily northern New Mexico and southern Colorado. Penitentes, commonly known as *Los Hermanos Penitentes* (The Penitent Brothers) or simply *Los Hermanos* (The Brothers), are almost exclusively men of Hispanic descent and Catholic faith. In time, localized associations of these men — originally organized for pious observances involving the expiation of sin through prayer and bodily penance, and for mutual aid — acquired judicial and political influence. Besides functioning as an integrative social power in isolated communities, these fraternities also became a conservative cultural force — preserving language, lore, customs, and faith, especially in poorer rural and urban areas of predominately Hispanic population. Now a secret religious society of restricted membership and indeterminate influence, the *Cofradías* (Confraternities) or *Hermandades* (Brotherhoods) formerly served as the nucleus of a folk religion in the fullest sense.

Unfortunately, most accounts of Penitente activities reflect prejudice, bias, and insufficient information. Derivative studies often compound these faults by uncritically compiling previous sources. Much of the confusion results from inadequate understanding of the Brotherhood's history and beliefs. Undue emphasis on severe penitential activities of self-flagellation and simulated crucifixion also distorts the image usually presented. It is necessary to counteract these inaccurate views with balanced historical and functional interpretations.

A second important problem is the lack of "inside" perspective and primary field studies. Few trained participant-observers have attempted to study a Penitente community, and relatively few Spanish-Americans have themselves reported on or interpreted the Brotherhood. This is understandable in the case of Brothers pledged to secrecy. However, it does mean that fresh insights, suggested by accounts of persons intimately associated with active Brotherhoods, are not generated. Facts and hypotheses are hard to check. Consequently, a full picture of the actual daily and annual workings of a Penitente community of worship and mutual aid is difficult to assemble.

Nonetheless, perhaps the best overall perspective on the Penitentes is as a folk religion with unique historical and sociocultural complexities. This designation is not derogatory in the slightest. The term denotes a traditional, relatively unorganized system of religious beliefs, symbols, and practices shared on a community level. These are clearly related to the theology, liturgy, and hierarchy of the official religion, but the exact relationship is variable. Thus, e.g., the local folk religion may coexist with the more universal religion, or it may be in active tension with current, official doctrine and practice. In fact, throughout their history, the Penitentes have had to accommodate to changes in Church and State policies while maintaining rituals and activities satisfactory to their own spiritual and social needs. It is therefore impossible to describe a single typical Brotherhood or even a set of rituals without first considering the vicissitudes of the Society's history.

HISTORICAL ASPECTS

Because of the Spanish drive for spiritual as well as material conquest, missionaries always took part in military expeditions – in the case of New Mexico, beginning with Coronado's 1540-1541 explorations. Franciscans accompanied the first party of colonizers, led by Don Juan de Oñate, in 1598. (Their settlement, near San Juan Pueblo, was moved to present-day Santa Fe in 1610.) All missionaries in the new, remote frontier were Franciscans. After the Pueblo Revolt in 1680 and the Spanish retreat to El Paso, Franciscans accompanied Don Diego de Vargas when he reconquered the area, 1692-1694. From that time and throughout the 18th century, an inadequate number of *frailes* (friars) established missions among the Indians *and* administered to the Spanish settlers, most of whom lived in a few towns along the upper Rio Grande, with main population centers at Santa Fe, Santa Cruz, and Albuquerque.

In the first two centuries of Spanish rule, New Mexico was administered by royal authority and the Franciscan Order of Friars Minor, i.e., by a Church-State system. The Custodian, head of the Franciscan Order in New Mexico, was also prelate of the Church, with limited episcopal powers. Increasingly, however, the Bishop of Durango (Mexico) pressed for episcopal jurisdiction. He prevailed, and, in 1797, villa churches at Santa Cruz, Santa Fe, Albuquerque, and El Paso were secularized by *curas* (priests) responsible to Durango. Although Franciscans remained with the missions, after Mexico declared independence from Spain in 1821, the friars lost royal financial support and were forced out, a withdrawal virtually complete by 1840.

Religion was by this time in a deplorable state, with the few priests charging exorbitant fees to perform rites of baptism, confirmation, matrimony, and burial. This deterioration worsened with the population and territorial expansion under Mexican rule. It was during the so-called Secular Period (c. 1790-1850), then, that the Penitentes grew strong, thereby fulfilling important needs for spiritual solace and collective survival in a semiarid environment amid still-hostile nomadic Indians.

Theories of Origin

The precise origin of the Penitente Brotherhood still remains obscure. Both Woodward (34) and Chávez (8) have assembled evidence refuting and supporting the various sources suggested, primarily by early American writers and by the American ecclesiastical authorities, who in 1851 took control of the Catholic Church in the annexed territory. The main theories and arguments are briefly discussed below:

1. *Indian influence.* Shocked by what they considered "primitive" self-tortures, and impressed by the superficial similarity of the *morada* (Penitente meeting-place) to the Indians' kiva, some writers attempted to prove that Indians influenced Penitente rites. The main suggestions were:

(a)   Blood penances and sacrifices of the Mexican Aztecs were assimilated by the conquering Spanish culture and spread to remote areas such as New Mexico.

(b)   Customs of New Mexican Indians during the historical period, e.g., tribal penance and whipping, were adopted by settlers isolated from centers of Church authority.

(c)   Indian "death worship" became a part of Penitente rites, which did include *memento mori* such as the death cart.

In all cases, fuller knowledge of Indian and Spanish cultural history proved the fallacy of such hypotheses. Indeed, the main influences were if anything the other way around — from the dominant Spanish *to* the subordinated Indians.

2. *Survival of medieval 'Flagellanti'.* Supposedly initiated by St. Anthony of Padua in the early 13th century, bands of flagellants appeared at various times during the Middle Ages. In 1260, after the

wars of the Guelfs and Ghibellines and the plague of 1259, processions of self-punishing *disciplinati* were reorganized by Raniero Fansani, an Umbrian hermit. Opposed by the Church as heretical sects, these groups reappeared during the plague years of the Black Death (1348-1350) and spread throughout Europe, despite further ecclesiastical condemnation. Not to be confused with Church-directed, lay associations for penance, such as were especially common from about 1350 through 1600, these fanatical groups gradually disappeared during the Renaissance. Spain, however, was neither politically nor religiously united until the late 15th century, and the populace, involved in religious crusades against the Moors, was not as affected by Italian and later European penitential frenzies of the 13th and 14th centuries. In any case, a strong influence has so far not been proved. The position that the New Mexican Penitentes represent a direct survival of these medieval *Flagellanti* is not yet tenable.

3. *Religious plays for drama and didacticism.* Religious plays *(autos sacramentales)* had developed in Spain by the 15th century, and flowered in the 16th and early 17th centuries. Originally part of Corpus Christi celebrations, they were eventually performed on Christmas, Epiphany, Easter, and saints' days. In the New World, Franciscan missionaries (and later those from other Orders) composed *autos* in native languages or translated and adapted Spanish ones for evangelization and instruction. In addition, the Spanish colonials themselves maintained certain traditional Spanish *autos,* likewise with Church approbation. These plays were carried north by the colonization movement and gradually became part of the folk culture in outpost communities, where copybook versions of some old *autos* are still extant. However, few passion plays, like the one presented annually at Tomé, New Mexico, or the Talpa (New Mexico) version staged by the Penitentes, have survived. While it is likely that the Brotherhoods appropriated portions of such plays, the fundamental worship complex of realistic enactment, intimate participation, and belief in salvation through bodily penance is a deeper, more pervasive dramatic and religious configuration. The traditional mystery plays are possible sources only for elements of the Penitente rituals, not for the basic system of religious beliefs and practices.

4. *Outgrowth of the Third Order of St. Francis.* Third Orders are lay

associations approved and governed by Catholic Church authorities. Members meeting admission requirements must go through a novitiate and afterwards make a profession of observing the Order's Rule of Life. There are no public vows or community life, and members strive to lead a more perfect Christian life while maintaining a secular existence. Members of any of the four Tertiary Orders may belong to any number of confraternities, which do not rank as high as Third Orders.

St. Francis of Assisi established a First Order, the Friars Minor, with rules approved by Pope Innocent III in 1210, and a Second Order, the Sisters of Clare or Poor Clares, in 1212. According to tradition, he developed the idea of a Third Order Secular while preaching in Cannara, where the entire village wished to abandon their homes and follow him. Original rules for the Tertiaries were drawn up by Francis and Cardinal Ugolino (later Pope Gregory IX) in 1221, but the only extant document is the Capistran Rule, dated 1228. The more familiar Rule of the Third Order was approved by Pope Nicholas IV in 1289, and prescribes organization, administration (by the Friars Minor), and a life of simplicity, humility, peacefulness, and piety, within the secular world.

The existence of the Third Order of St. Francis in New Mexico is well documented at least from the time of de Vargas' reconquest, although the societies at Santa Fe, Santa Cruz, and Albuquerque did not always operate with a vigorous membership and the best of facilities. Salpointe notes that members celebrated private devotions and public feast days and that the privilege of wearing the modified Franciscan habit was granted at special masses and during Holy Week. Extant wills and other documents indicate that members were also buried in the Franciscan habit and white cord. Technically, the Order ceased to have canonical existence when the Franciscans were expelled and their missions secularized.

Many writers subscribe to the theory that the Penitentes developed out of these leaderless Third Orders. The Reverend Alexander M. Darley (9), a Presbyterian missionary in southern Colorado, and Charles Fletcher Lummis (24), a journalist and popularizer of the Southwest, were major early American proponents of this viewpoint. It was in fact the opinion of the Church itself, as represented by Archbishop Lamy and his successor Archbishop Salpointe. At various times, these authorities attempted to impose Third Order Rules upon the Brotherhood, but they encountered resistance from deeply devout Penitentes convinced that their practices were consonant with an old Spanish Catholic heritage.

Arguments against this theory revolve around the dissimilarities between the Franciscan Third Order Rules and the Penitente confraternities' constitutions and by-laws. The former prescribe a way of life, while the latter are primarily concerned with the obligations of penance. Another confusion seems to have arisen due to the misreading of a 1794 document, which refers to the Tertiaries as *La Venerable Orden Tercera de Penitencia* (The Venerable Third Order of Penance, another name for it common almost since its inception), as indicating a Third Order of Penitentes. Since the theory is still commonly held, however, perhaps the best summary statement is the conclusion drawn by Reginald Fisher after examining "noninstitutionalized" elements of Franciscanism which survived the Secular Period:

> It is possible that during the latter part of the 19th century a fusion of the tertiary confraternities with penitential brotherhoods may have occurred. In such event the Third Order did carry through the secular period in the perverted form of tertiary-Franciscan-penitential-brotherhoods. However, present knowledge of the period is not sufficient to say what actually did happen to the Third Order confraternities during the secular interlude. In any event, a great amount of Franciscanism became incorporated in the attitudes and practices of *Los Hermanos Penitentes.* (11; p. 271)

5. *Penitential confraternities.* The most common official name for the Penitentes is *Cofradía de Nuestro Padre Jesús Nazareno.* Other titles include the words *unión, fraternidad, hermandad,* and *sociedad,* all of which, by Canon law, may refer to religious sodalities or pious associations of the faithful. Such societies are characteristic of Spanish Catholicism in its Old and New World manifestations.

During the Middle Ages in Europe, from about the 9th century on, pious brotherhoods and trade guilds became important religious-social-economic institutions. However, Spanish *cofradías* and *gremios* (trade guilds) did not develop until the late 12th century. They operated according to rules (as to purposes, rights, and obligations) in *ordenanzas* (ordinances) issued by Church, royal, or municipal authority. Although at first interrelated, the two types of association grew apart. The *gremio* acquired political power, which forced its persecution and abolition, but confraternities for pious ends and mutual aid continued to be sanctioned, and proliferated in the 15th and 16th centuries. Because Spain was not affected by the Reformation, *hermandades* remained important until the 18th century, and exist in attenuated form today. From the first, these *cofradías* were also established in the New World, where they eventually assumed variant forms among conquering, native, and *mestizo* (mixed) populations.

In addition to cults of the Passion, the Virgin, patron saints, and Death, sacramental confraternities devoted to penance also developed and combined with other societies and observances in the complex of Spanish Catholicism. Penance is one of the four Church Sacraments instituted by Christ. Intensified penance through corporal mortification has been a part of Christianity from its inception. The motives for penance are usually given as:

(a)   the reparation of personal and other sins
(b)   the demonstration of devotion to Christ by imitation, as in the following New Testament teachings:
      Luke 9.23 (RSV): "And he said to all, 'If any man would come after me, let him deny himself and take up his cross daily and follow me.' "
      I Peter 2.21 (RSV): "For to this you have been called, because Christ also suffered for you, leaving you an example, that you should follow in his steps."
(c)   the mastery of human passions through self-discipline, according to St. Paul's letter:
      I Corinthians 9.27 (RSV): "but I pommel my body and subdue it, lest after preaching to others I myself should be disqualified."

The forms through which these motives find expression — whether solemnized, public, private, severe or mild — vary from place to place and century to century.

In Spain, manifestations of penitential spirit tended to be public, dramatic, realistic, and severe. Processions of flagellants — both token (over clothes) and actual self-scourgers — were common. During Holy Week, processions of *cofrades* (brothers), whipping, carrying crosses, dragging chains, and so on, followed others who bore realistic *pasos* (figures or sculptured groups depicting aspects of the Passion), often along outdoor routes representing the *Via Crucis* (Way of the Cross). Many of these rituals are still observed in modified form by Sevillian penitential societies. The spirit and practices of such demonstrations were maintained in the New World by the Spanish colonials.

Penitential discipline was familiar to and practiced by the Spanish colonists in New Mexico. The best-known early references to the custom of self-flagellation are found in Villagrá's epic poem chronicling Oñate's expedition and in Benavides' 1630 report on his dual service as custodian-prelate of the New Mexican Church and commissary of the Inquisition. On March 20, 1598, somewhere south of present-day El Paso, Texas, Oñate's party celebrated Good Friday by prayer and penance, including public self-flagellation, while Oñate scourged himself in a private act of contrition. On April 4, 1627, in a pueblo southeast of Albuquerque, Fray Alonso de Benavides was upbraided by an Indian for being one of the "crazy" Spaniards who whipped themselves publicly. The accusation drew no more than passing comment in Benavides' *Memorial.* Unfortunately, after the Reconquest, since most attention was concentrated on converting and governing the Indians, references and documents relating to customs and rituals of the Spanish colonists are very sparse. This has led to speculation about possible Third Order origins of the Penitentes, as well as to two theories involving *cofradías de penitencia* (penitential confraternities). These are as follows:

A. *An internal development out of a continuing confraternity tradition.* Convinced that there are enough 17th and 18th century references to New Mexican confraternities to substantiate their continued importance as an integrative socioreligious force, Woodward (34) claims that the Penitentes developed from this unbroken tradition. These associations, so characteristic of 16th-century Spain, were retained by isolated colonists nostalgic for familiar religious traditions and in need of mutual benefit and social controls. That penitential activities as such or specific names referring to penance are not recorded is consonant with the fact that Spanish colonial rituals and customs were taken for granted throughout these two centuries.

B. *A late transplant from outside New Mexico.* Chávez (8) insists on specific references to the Brotherhood for historical evidence. Fray Francisco Atanasio Domínguez' thorough 1776 report on religion in New Mexico makes no mention of penitential societies. The first reference to a "Brotherhood of Penitentes" does not appear until

STONE *MORADA* at Tecolote, New Mexico.

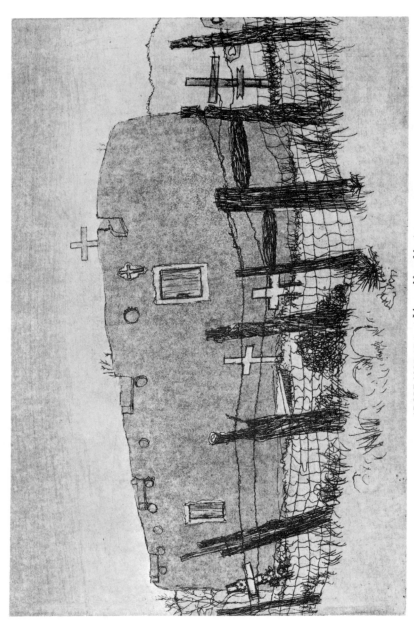

ADOBE MORADA at Llano, New Mexico.

Bishop Zubiria's denunciation of them, dated July 21, 1833, from Santa Cruz. By correlating this with other data — especially the fact that the Penitentes emerge "full-blown," with terminology, organization, and rites nearly identical to those of 16th-century Penitentes of Seville — Chávez concludes that a person or persons from the south (or possibly a book describing such societies and rituals) introduced the Brotherhood into the Santa Cruz area, which includes the famous Chimayó pilgrimage center and the important *genízaro* (non-Pueblo Indian captives who spoke Spanish and were semi-Christianized) village of Abiquiú. Local variations accrued, and the organization quickly spread to fill the void left by departing Franciscans.

Resolution of the origins question is probably unlikely. Nevertheless, whatever their beginnings, the Penitente Brotherhoods are clearly *not* aberrant. They exist well within the history of Spanish Catholicism and its mystical, penitential, and Franciscan traditions. Maintained by colonists isolated in a hostile frontier with a climate similar to their Spanish homeland, it is not at all surprising that this is so.

Later History
Until the early 19th century, New Mexico continued relatively unchanged — an isolated agrarian society dependent upon Spanish and Mexican inspiration and administration. With the opening of the Santa Fe Trail in 1821, trappers, traders, explorers, and other travelers, predominately French Canadians and Anglo-Americans, filtered into the region. Brigadier General Stephen Watts Kearny entered Santa Fe on August 18, 1846, claiming New Mexico as a territory of the United States. Aside from the 1847 Taos Rebellion, there was little active opposition to this conquest. Hispanic life continued much as usual, and settlements in southern Colorado were established in the early 1850's.

By 1863, following the Treaty of Guadalupe Hidalgo (1848), the Gadsden Purchase (1853), and several Congressional bills, most of the territory covered by present-day New Mexico had been established. A number of official military expeditions had explored the region, preparing the way for post-Civil War settlers. Changes came about slowly, however, and Anglos (i.e., non-Hispanic and non-Indian peoples) did not arrive in large numbers until after the railroads were completed (1878-1911) and the nomadic Indians subdued. Colorado had meantime become the thirty-eighth state on August 1, 1876. By the time the Territory of New Mexico was admitted to the Union as the forty-seventh state, on January 6, 1912, many factors had altered the fabric of Hispanic village life, not the least of these being the influx of Protestants and the establishment of public and parochial education.

Although some writers claim that nativistic reaction to Anglo conquest resulted in more excessive Penitente rites, there seems to be little evidence to substantiate such an intensification. The main changes were in the Brotherhood's status with respect to Church and government, and in expanded concerns in the newly-secularized spheres of law and politics. Clearly, membership provided a familiar haven for the new United States citizens, thus preserving much of the Spanish cultural heritage. However, Penitentes were not necessarily conservative to the point of fanatic nativism, and to a certain extent helped in the adaptation to a new government and a dominant culture which was not exclusively Catholic or even Spanish-speaking.

The newly-established Church hierarchy regarded the Penitentes as a problematic phenomenon, initially rebuking and finally denouncing them. In 1850, Pope Pius IX named Santa Fe the center of a Southwest diocese and appointed John B. Lamy as Vicar-Apostolic. Bishop Lamy arrived in 1851 with three French priests. The new, alien clergy felt that the Penitentes were contrary to modern ecclesiastical order and harmful to the image of Catholicism in the eyes of newcomers from the East.

Although loose documents in the Archives of the Archdiocese of Santa Fe include approved Penitente rulebooks from as early as 1853, Lamy did not issue official *arreglos* (rules) for the Brotherhood until March 9, 1857, and again on June 8, 1858. Basically, these guidelines are concerned with the Brothers' observing secret, moderate penances, leading good Catholic lives, and maintaining strict respect for and obedience to the immediate authority of the *Hermano Mayor* (Elder Brother, in charge of the *morada* and all its activities) and the ultimate rule of the Church. Lamy apparently instituted the practice of "verification," whereby a parishioner had to deny or affirm *and* denounce Penitente membership before he could receive the Sacraments.

Chávez (8) also claims that Lamy succeeded in convincing both the public and the Penitentes themselves that the Brotherhood had evolved from the Third Order of St. Francis. Lamy became Archbishop in 1875, and retired in July, 1885, leaving the task of disciplining the Penitentes to his successor, Archbishop John B. Salpointe.

The religious scene during Salpointe's reign was further complicated by increasing Protestant strength in the region. Priests in northern villages had to obey the circulars from Santa Fe while vying for their parishioners' loyalties with evangelical missionaries. Nonetheless, the new Archbishop steadfastly continued his efforts to make the Penitentes "return" to the Third Order. A circular of 1886 included copies of the Third Order Rules (those approved by Pope Leo XIII in 1883) for distribution to the various *Hermanos Mayores.* Public flagellation and cross-carrying were prohibited. During the first Synod of the Archdiocese of Santa Fe, in June, 1888, Salpointe further condemned the Penitentes. Priests were ordered to refuse to celebrate Mass in chapels belonging to practicing Brothers and to deny Sacraments to those who ignored the 1886 circular and still held the old wakes for the dead. A circular dated March 31, 1889, reiterated the Third Order origins, denounced flagellant sects, and denied the Sacraments to any who practiced flagellation or cross-carrying in public. Yet another Salpointe circular threatening the Penitentes was dated February 7, 1892. The effect of all these was less a reformation of the Brotherhood than a deepened secrecy, even after further threats in 1899, under Archbishop Peter Bourgade.

The Church condemned the Penitentes for their seeming disregard of "proper" authority, their secrecy, their too-rigorous penitential practices, their political involvement, and, presumably, for the unfavorable light they cast on Catholicism as a whole. In actuality, however, relations were perhaps more amicable, with priests overlooking certain Holy Week practices of otherwise loyal parishioners. The possibility that Church opposition was more in the interests of a good public image than a purge against the Brotherhood has in fact been suggested by Mary Austin in manuscript notes on Lee's thesis (22). Whatever the truth in such an allegation, it remains clear that neither Church representatives nor local Brothers were diametrically opposed. Not all *moradas* espoused the more zealous rites, and not all parish priests considered themselves above compromise.

Besides the loss of unqualified Church support, the new American regime also meant that the Penitentes had to function under a government in which church and state were separate institutions. Because of this, a series of laws were enacted, incorporating various Brotherhoods as benevolent societies with certain legal rights. The first of these was passed on January 30, 1861, as "An Act to incorporate the 'Pious Fraternity of the County of Taos' " (an area which then included most of northern New Mexico). Further legislation regarding "corporations not organized for profit" was enacted fairly regularly. One of the most important acts was passed on February 20, 1915, as Chapter 6 of the *1915 Session Laws of the State of New Mexico* — a bill defining as criminal libel the publication of intentionally malicious material concerning any fraternal or religious order or society. Thus, by the time their legal status was secured, many Penitentes had acquired both political and judicial expertise within the new system.

Documentation supporting claims of Penitente complicity in judicial decisions or political elections has always been difficult to produce. For example, many writers conjecture that the Penitentes were among those behind the Taos Rebellion of 1847. Padre Antonio José Martínez, the dynamic and schismatic Taos priest who had much influence over the Brothers, is also implicated, although his guilt has never been proved. Another implicated priest, José Manuel Gallegos of Albuquerque, also unfrocked by Bishop Lamy, was nonetheless elected territorial delegate to the United States Congress, possibly with Penitente support. Since that time, many partially true speculations about the secret Brotherhood's secular activities have persisted.

Local justice traditionally had been administered by the Penitentes themselves, generally in an informal court hearing presided over by the *Hermano Mayor*. Often, offenses could be expiated in religious acts of self-inflicted penances. When the jury system was introduced and cases tried in secular courts, the transition proved difficult. Brothers sworn to protect fellow members and to abide by the decisions of their own officers did not always make impartial jurors. For many years, charges and countercharges of unfair trials due to Penitente solidarity were rife, continuing well into the 20th century.

The political activities of the Penitentes have been analyzed somewhat better. The most popular view contends that the various *moradas* provided large blocs of votes easily influenced by the simple expedient of the politician's undergoing a mild initiation and token self-punishment. Another opinion holds that the Republican party controlled most Penitente votes. In a case study of certain elections in San Miguel County, New Mexico, a strong Penitente area, Holmes found only some truth in either notion. His analysis (17; pp. 38-49) shows that the Penitente vote was somewhat significant, predominately Republican, but neither opportunistic nor invariable. Further, campaigns were in keeping with the techniques of persuasion and shrewd politicking characteristic of most Spanish-American political participation. Still another popular belief — that occasionally the same village supported both Democratic and Republican *moradas* — has not always proved true, as, e.g., Ahlborn discovered in Abiquiú (1; p. 136). While the Brotherhood no doubt suffered because of political factionalism, in the long run, such involvement fulfilled at least some of the need for adequate Spanish-American representation.

By the time of the Depression, membership in the Brotherhood had declined, although the Penitentes were still strong in rural areas and among the poorer urban residents. Increased prejudice and severe economic pressure aggravated the plight of all "natives," but no studies have shown whether, for example, there were differences in the relief measures necessary for Penitente (mutual aid) and non-Penitente communities. In any case, important changes were taking place within the overall structure of the Brotherhood itself.

The key figure in these movements was Don Miguel Archibeque, a longtime Santa Fe resident. Archibeque, born July 1, 1883, was initiated into the *Hermandad* during Holy Week of 1910. He devoted much of his life to modifying and organizing the Brotherhood in order to bring it back under Church direction.

Prior to the 1930's, individual *moradas* usually operated as autonomous units with only unofficial, friendly relations with other nearby groups. In April, 1931, a county organization, *La Fraternidad de Nuestro Padre Jesús del Condado de Taos,* was incorporated, with a *concilio* (council) of local *Hermanos Mayores* and other elected representatives. It was governed by an elected *Hermano Mayor Principal.* Other such organizations were established elsewhere. Despite these early attempts at order, there was still bitter disagreement about the return to the Church, and it was eight years after Church recognition before the last *moradas* joined the newly-sanctioned Brotherhood.

In a statement signed and dated January 28, 1947, Archbishop Edwin V. Byrne formally recognized "the Brothers of Jesus of Nazareth (commonly called the Penitentes)" as a pious Catholic society of obscure origins and a partially dubious history. Byrne cited Archibeque's efforts to abolish political and penitential abuses, and agreed to guide the Brotherhood himself. He declared: (1) that the Penitentes were not a fanatical sect; (2) that they were related to the Third Order of St. Francis and organized to attain salvation through penance; (3) that penances were to be modified and private; and (4) that the Church had absolute authority over the Brotherhood. The Archbishop appointed Archibeque to assume the duties of *Hermano Supremo.* Other officials were to be elected annually.

As of 1960, Holmes (17; p. 38) estimates Penitente membership at perhaps two or three thousand Brothers associated with some 135 *moradas.* Such figures are at best tenuous. More credence can be attached to overall organizational details. Holmes reports nine New Mexico *concilios* (districts) in San Miguel, Mora, Taos, and Rio Arriba counties, with isolated *moradas* directly supervised by the *Hermano Supremo.* Main Colorado membership centers around Walsenburg and in the San Luis Valley. A general meeting and election is held annually at Santa Fe. Attended by all *Hermanos Mayores* and their *concilio* representatives, it is formally addressed by the Archbishop and other Church officials. Recognition has thus been complete.

The Penitentes have played an integral part in a complex regional history of tri-cultural confrontation. The outlines of the Brotherhood's development are reasonably clear, but the unique intricacies and local details remain secret. This secrecy has been in large part self-protective, but it is also an important aspect of the Brothers' deep religious beliefs, of their faith and the faith of their communities. Perhaps this is best expressed in the words of the late Archbishop Edwin V. Byrne. In 1958, a limited edition of a book entitled *The Way of the Cross: A New Mexico Version* (Reginald Fisher, ed.) was published. It contained the music and words to four old Penitente *alabados* (hymns) and the accompanying service. Byrne presented a copy of this volume to Archibeque. The inscription (according to *Time,* September 1, 1958) read:

For Don Miguel Archibeque . . . in appreciation of the important role his Brotherhood has had in the development and preservation of this beautiful expression of the true vocation of New Mexico Spanish people.

RITUAL ASPECTS

The Penitente Brotherhoods are legally incorporated, nonprofit benevolent associations. Now, they are also organized religious fraternities under Church authority. Historically, they viewed themselves as an obedient group of *Hermanos* serving their community and their faith through worship and mutual aid. Their purpose was to maintain a Christian Brotherhood in order better to imitate the life and death of Jesus and to sustain more perfect fraternal relations among members, and, through them, within their families and communities.

The rules and rituals of the local chapters (i.e., *moradas*) were designed to further these ends. Details of their customs varied greatly from village to village. This is to be expected, with communication as difficult as it was, and in view of the various intervillage rivalries and affinities. Structurally, however, there is a certain basic procedural and ritual pattern which can be abstracted from the many accounts and eyewitness reports. The descriptions that follow, then, are roughly characteristic of Penitente practices in the early 20th century. They are intended as helpful, composite orderings, and should not be read as exact reports of a specific organization and set of observances. In general, though, they describe typical activities of the Penitentes about this time, and, to a certain extent, today.

Local Organization

The Penitente *morada* was organized into a hierarchy of male members somewhat like the informal ranking among siblings in the traditional Hispanic family. According to Edmonson, "the Hispano system resolves conflicts between siblings by a hierarchical principle, in which older siblings achieve quasi-parental status and younger siblings are expected to submit" (10; p. 64). Among the Brothers, highest authority was granted to the *Hermano Mayor,* who was usually elected annually. He took responsibility for the overall workings of the organization, for all meetings and observances, for every member, and even for fulfilling certain community expectations. Occasionally, there was also an *Hermano Segundo* (Second Brother) to assist the Elder Brother. In any case, the year-round power of the *Hermano Mayor* was considerable, and he enjoyed a high status in the community.

Other officers were also elected annually from among the *Hermanos de Luz* (Brothers of Light), who had undergone up to five years of Lenten penitential exercises as *Hermanos de Sangre* (Brothers of Blood), and were thus full-fledged, "cleansed" members. These officials and their duties usually included:

(a) *Celador* (Warden): maintains order within and outside the *morada;* administers punishments; sergeant-at-arms.

(b) *Secretario* (Clerk): custodian of records and rule book, from which he reads upon request.

(c) *Mandatorio* (Agent, sometimes called Collector or Treasurer): notifies members of duties, meetings, ceremonies, etc.; collects dues or alms; instructs novices.

(d) *Maestro de Novios* (Teacher of the Novices): examines all novices petitioning for admission and supervises their instruction by the *Mandatorio.*

(e) *Sangrador,* or *Picador* (Blood-letter, or Pricker): inflicts the seal of the Brotherhood (three horizontal and three vertical gashes across the back) on those preparing for penitential exercises; whips the novices.

(f) *Rezador* (Reader, i.e., one who prays; also called *Rogador,* or Petitioner): reads prayers and rituals from a copybook containing various texts and orders of service; takes an important role in most ceremonies. Some sources say there is also a *Cantador* (Singer) to lead the hymns.

(g) *Pitero* (Piper): plays the *pito* (homemade flute) as musical accompaniment for various services, *never* for pleasure.

(h) *Coadjutor* (Assistant): washes the whips; attends to the wounds of Brothers performing penances.

(i) *Enfermero* (Nurse): cares for sick members and does various charitable acts in the community throughout the year.

In addition, *Ayudantes* (Helpers) or *Acompañadores* (Attendants), representing Simon the Cyrenian, were appointed to accompany, and if necessary aid, each whipper and cross-bearer. During Holy Week, different *Mayordomos* (Stewards) were assigned or self-appointed to supply meals for Brothers in the *morada.* Stewards were not necessarily members, and other religious persons in the community often offered food as a pious act.

PROCESIÓN DEL ESTANDARTE

The photographs on the following pages come from the Collections in the Museum of New Mexico, and are reproduced by courtesy of the Museum of New Mexico, Santa Fe. The negatives are part of the Kow-ina Foundation collection, and were loaned to the Museum by the Kow-ina Cultural Research Foundation, Inc., which also supplied the accompanying information. Although the pilgrimage depicted is somewhat unusual, the pictures vividly illustrate the solemn ritual of a devout people.

In the *Procesión del Estandarte* (Procession of the Standard), Brothers from Cuba, New Mexico, made a pilgrimage on foot which lasted several weeks. They walked to San Ysidro, where there was a ceremony in the *morada,* to Marquez (then known as Juan Tafoya), to Moquino, to Cubero, and on to St. John's, Arizona. On the return trip, they were supposed to have stopped at San Mateo and Cabezon, but this is not certain. The practice was discontinued about 1912.

The four photographs in the center fold (pp. 22-23) were taken by Emil Bibo in April, *c.* 1908. They show the reception of the *Hermanos* from Cuba by the Brothers from Cubero, just north of the village.

(a) p. 22, *upper photo* (no. 44900): The arrival of the *Hermanos* from Cuba, New Mexico, at Cubero, New Mexico.
(b) p. 22, *lower photo* (no. 44902): A close-up of the meeting between the Brothers from Cuba (with identifying ribbons) and those from Cubero. Casiano Baca, the *Hermano Mayor* from Cubero, is kneeling at the far left. The white-bearded man standing at the far right is the *Celador,* Francisco Duran. Other persons are also identified by name in the explanatory text from the Kow-ina Foundation. (Note the musicians standing amid the kneeling Brothers.)
(c) p. 23, *upper photo* (no. 44898): A view of the Procession from behind the Cubero contingent.
(d) p. 23, *lower photo* (no. 44899): The entire group outside the village limits, with Mount Taylor in the distance. (Note the girls in white and the traditional black *rebozos,* or shawls, worn by the women.)

The photograph on p. 24 (no. 44906), is by Lee Marmon, Laguna, New Mexico, 1963. It shows a *descanso* and cross sacred to the settlement of Piedra Lumbre. On a small knoll beside the road between Piedra Lumbre and Moquino, it used to mark the resting place for funeral processions walking to the cemetery at Moquino or Cebolleta. The Procession of the Standard stopped to worship at this marker.

Men seeking admission into the Society had to have the consent of parents and/or spouse. During a designated novitiate, which may have been preceded by an *entrega,* or "surrender" to the Brotherhood, novices were carefully instructed and their lives thoroughly examined. Presumably, sometime during his first *entrada* (entrance), the *novio* took an oath pledging himself to secrecy and loyalty. The exact details of the initiation are not clear because they seem to coincide with the entrance ceremonies followed by all who intended to perform bodily penances during that particular Holy Week. In any case, the first administration of the Seal of Obligation and the swearing of the oath would probably constitute a formal initiation. Full membership was attained only after several years of penitential activities, and might at any time be denied for various misdeeds. If expulsion followed conviction, membership could not be regained; otherwise, full status might be redeemed through renewed penitential exercises. Occasionally too, a Brother of Light might feel a personal need to do severe penance, and requested permission from the *Hermano Mayor.* Still, despite the obscurity surrounding the exact differences between initiation and preparation for penance, it is clear that such procedures existed. They accentuated the Brotherhood's solidarity, as well as its religious purposes of struggling to attain salvation through penance, prayer, and meditation.

Women may sometimes have been members of a Brotherhood, but it is more likely that they generally served as auxiliaries — preparing meals, cleaning the *morada,* caring for the sick, helping at *velorios* (wakes or vigils), and following public processions. Though private, their penances — e.g., crawling to the *Calvario* on their knees, walking with *arroz* (rice) in their shoes, and so on — might be relatively no less severe. Wallrich (33) describes southern Colorado organizations of these *auxiliadoras* (female auxiliaries) in some detail. Since there is little corroborative evidence from New Mexico, the complexity of the association may be local. Also, women's groups related to the Penitentes should not be confused with the various Church societies common to the region. In any case, women almost invariably played subordinate, supportive roles with respect to the male cadre of the Brotherhood.

Locally, then, *moradas* were structured to maintain a strict internal organization, to observe certain rituals of worship both public and private, and to assure mutual aid and community benefits. The analogy to the family is apparent. Indeed, Mills and Grove characterize the Brotherhood as "a supplementary family" (26; p. 38). By providing earthly protection and spiritual guidance, this "family" nurtured and sustained its members through all manner of adversity.

Ritual Observances

In a study based on field work in northwestern New Mexico, Edmonson gives a cogent summary of the larger religious context of Penitentism:

> . . . the religious life of the Hispanos is a blend of Roman Catholic and secular Spanish elements with a religious fraternity [the Penitentes] and an assemblage of magical witchcraft and curing practices. Its biggest ceremonials are the life crises of initiation, marriage and death, and the calendric observances of the Fiesta and Holy Week. Its role structure is simple, focussing on the padre [priest], the mayordomo [steward for the local church] and the compadrazgo [godparent or sponsor] system, and its symbolism is the dramatic and elaborate hagiology of the European Catholic tradition. Its cosmology builds on the basic teachings of the Roman Catholic church, with a strong emphasis on acceptance of the 'natural order' ordained by the will of God. (10; p. 44)

Within this context, good *Católicos* (Catholics), including Penitentes, abided by the Ten Commandments, and, whenever possible, the six chief Commandments of the Holy Mother Church, which decree: 1) assistance at Mass on Sundays and holydays of obligation; 2) fasting and abstinence on appointed days; 3) confession of sins at least once a year; 4) Holy Communion during the Easter time; 5) contribution to Church support; 6) observance of Church laws concerning matrimony. The Apostles' Creed, certain prayers, and the Church Sacraments complete the nucleus of this belief complex. It formed the basis for the Penitentes' faith, which they expressed in ways not always congenial to prevailing doctrine, but which were developed when the Church inadequately served the region.

According to Foster (13; p. 158), religion in Spain is best considered as comprising the basic cult of the seven Church Sacraments (Baptism, Confirmation, Matrimony, Holy Orders, Holy Eucharist, Penance, and Extreme Unction) and the specialized cults of Christ, Mary, and the saints, with all their associated feast days, pilgrimages, dramas, legends, and sundry popular beliefs. Much of this was transplanted to the New World:

If we look at the basic pattern of fiestas in Hispanic America, as manifest in all countries, the picture is surprisingly similar: Epiphany, Candlemas, Lent, Holy Week, Corpus Christi, All Saints' and All Souls' days, and Christmas, plus a fiesta, usually for the patron saint of the community. Presumably these are the feast days the Church considered central to dogma, and the activities of each were thought best calculated to educate Indians in the new faith, as well as to maintain the faith of Iberian settlers. In one part or another of America other customs occur . . . They are, in contrast to the central dogma and the annual fiesta cycle, best thought of as resulting from informal transmission processes. (13; pp. 165-166)

These general patterns have also prevailed in the Hispanic Southwest, where the observances were often sponsored by the Penitentes themselves.

The Brotherhood was clearly most important during Lenten and Holy Week rituals. They also took part in funerals, especially those of dead Brothers. Other regular meetings may have been held in the beginning of May, on Corpus Christi, on August 15th (Assumption Day), on All Saints' and All Souls' Days (November 1st and 2nd), and on the day of the *morada's* patron saint. In addition, the Brothers often played important roles in the fiesta for the village patron saint. On special days, the *morada* chapel would be open to all worshippers, and services might be held. The *morada* might also serve as the *depósito* (repository) of the village *santos* (sacred images), from which they were carried on special occasions and at times of illness or mourning. In other words, the Brothers frequently supplied the practical organization behind various important observances and made available an appropriate physical setting, including singers and readers, for those who wished to worship.

The main ritual observances of the Penitentes are briefly described below. One fact should be emphasized, namely: that the Brothers never usurped the priestly functions of administering the Sacraments. None of their observances ever violated the Church's principles in this regard.

Ceremonials at Death. If a priest were available, the rites of passage at death included the Last Sacrament, a wake, a requiem mass, burial in ground consecrated by the Church, and mourning, with a mass shortly after the funeral and a memorial mass (or novena) one year after the death. The Penitente rituals substituted a *rosario* (extended prayer service), generally in the *morada,* for the Last

Sacrament. During the *velorio de difunto* (wake for the dead), Brothers took turns maintaining a vigil over the body, while the *Rezador* or *Cantador* chanted prayers and sang until dawn. Sometimes, the body was taken to the *morada* for a brief service. It was also common for Brothers to form a flagellant procession, whipping themselves as they circled the body, thus helping the journey of the dead Brother's soul. Another *rosario* replaced the requiem mass, and the body was not necessarily buried in consecrated ground. Commonly, Penitentes, like non-Penitentes who made a promise and requested burial *sin cajon* (without a coffin), were interred without a casket. Again, *rosarios* took the place of memorial services.

Non-Penitentes could request the Brotherhood's assistance in times of bereavement. The Brothers charitably contributed such services as *rosarios, velorios,* and grave digging, thus aiding poorer families unable to afford Church fees. In earlier days, when the Church was unavailable, the Brotherhood's spiritual and material contributions gave immeasurable solace.

A number of misconceptions are associated with Penitente customs at death. One involves the *descansos,* or piles of stones, sometimes marked with a small wooden cross or a carved stone marker, which are seen throughout the countryside. These do not mark Penitente graves — either of Brothers who died naturally or those who perished as a result of their part in the Holy Week rituals. They mark the places where processions of mourners bearing coffins to the *campo santo* (cemetery) rested and sang *alabados.* Believers stop at these *descansos,* say a *sudario* (prayer for the dead), and perhaps place another stone on the pile. A second custom, which is unconfirmed and likely legendary, involves the death of a Brother while enacting the *Cristo* (Christ) — a death which assures him salvation in Heaven. Supposedly, his relatives are notified when his shoes are placed on their doorstep, and the grave remains secret for one year following his demise. Others claim that he is buried upright, or a large cross and pile of rocks marks the spot. While there is a possibility that such practices have at least an earlier basis in fact, they seem to be more a part of the mystique outsiders project onto the secret Brotherhood.

La Cuaresma (Lent).　　Brothers meet on *Miércoles de Ceniza* (Ash Wednesday) and every Friday during Lent.

RITUAL EQUIPMENT. *Pito* (flute), *matraca* (clacker), *pedernales* (flints), *disciplina* (whip), *cuaderno* (copybook), candle-lantern of pierced tin, and *crucifijo* (crucifix).

CARVING DEPICTING A PENITENTIAL EXERCISE. A procession of *Rezador*, *Pitero*, flagellant, and cross-bearer approaches the *Calvario*. From the Collection of the Millicent A. Rogers Foundation Museum, Taos, New Mexico.

Public recitations of the Stations of the Cross are held, and at night there is generally a private flagellant procession. Fasting and sobriety prevail throughout the season. The requirement of at least annual Confession and Communion is usually met during this time.

La Semana Santa (Holy Week). The Brothers spend most of Holy Week in the *morada* — singing, praying, doing penances, sleeping (though not for extended periods) on the floor, and eating meals which are brought in to them. Breakfast is usually omitted, and the main food consumed is a highly nutritious, sweet substance called *panocha,* made from sprouted wheat flour boiled until thickened. As a rule, the men do not return home until officers for the coming year have been elected, either after the *Tinieblas* service or on the morning of Holy Saturday.

Martes Santo (Holy Tuesday). At night, novices and those Brothers who wish to do active penance make their ritual *entrada.* This involves a recited interchange between the Brothers within and the penitents outside. Inside, the penitent dons the *calzones* (white cotton trousers worn during penance) and approaches the assembled members. The *Sangrador* administers the six gashes of the *obligación,* and the penitent then begs forgiveness from each Brother. Sometimes, offended members give token lashes, but usually the *Celador* administers a suitable discipline. At other times, and this may be typical only of the novice's first initiation, the penitent calls for lashes from the *Sangrador* equal to the three meditations of the Passion, the five wounds of Christ, His seven last words, the forty days in the wilderness, and others, although he rarely stays conscious that long. The evening ends with hymns and prayers, while the *Coadjutor* bathes the penitents' wounds in an astringent of *romerillo* (silver sage).

El Ejercicio (Exercise). Penitential exercises were supervised by the *Hermano Mayor,* who granted permission for and sometimes even assigned them. Although decidedly severe, penances were not to be suicidal. Self-flagellation, either within the *morada* or in a procession, was most common. Brothers might also petition to drag a *madero* — a wooden cross taller than a man and often weighing several hundred pounds, carried with the cross-beam over the right shoulder. Sometimes, a man or men dragged the rock-filled death cart by means of a rope across the chest or over the shoulders and under the armpits. Other penances involving chains, cactus, or smaller crosses have been reported, and some say that Brothers of Light (in ordinary clothes) accompanying the penitents wore a circlet of thorns on their head. In any case, those punishing themselves publicly wore only the white *calzones* and a black *venda* (hood) covering the face. This was more to insure humility than to hide from authorities.

Active penitents formerly accompanied all the processions of Holy Week. In addition, smaller groups or single men might petition for permission to conduct an *ejercicio* to some local shrine or landmark. Their activities were accepted by the community, but their discipline was gradually disrupted by uncomprehending, horror-mongering new-comers. Penitential processions increasingly came to be held at night and in remote places. However, the Brothers' intense search for reparation and salvation continued, despite many reprehensible assaults on their privacy.

Miércoles Santo (Holy Wednesday). There are visits between *moradas*, as well as visits to the *morada* by non-Penitente worshippers. During *La Procesión de los Dolores* (The Procession of Sorrows), the Brothers walk from the *morada* to the *campo santo* or the *Calvario* (Calvary), a nearby hilltop marked by large crosses. They are led by the *Pitero*, the *Rezador*, the *Hermano Mayor*, and sometimes a member carrying a *crucifijo* (crucifix) or some other image as a guide. Women, children, and permitted visitors follow, as the Brothers observe *Las Estaciones* (The Stations of the Cross), which are generally marked by small wooden crosses along the route. *Alabados* and various prayers make up this devotion, which follows the fourteen stations of the Church *Via Crucis*.

Jueves Santo (Holy Thursday). The day is similar to the one preceding. In *La Procesión de la Santa Cruz* (The Procession of the Holy Cross), the Brother chosen to portray the *Cristo* appears, and there may be a dramatization of his seizure and trial before Pilate. The cherished role of Christ is granted by miracle, by lot, by decision of the officers, or by selection from among petitioners. Often, the dramatizations take place inside the *morada,* and the *Cristo* is reviled by his own Brothers.

Viernes Santo (Good Friday), or *Día de la Cruz* (Day of the Cross). Prayers, penances, and processions continue. About noon, there is a dramatization of the fourth station — *El Encuentro* (The Meeting) between Christ and His mother. All villagers participate. A group from the *morada* with an image of Christ meets a group from the church carrying a figure of the Virgin Mary, and an appropriate service follows. At two, there is another *Via Crucis* — *La Procesión de Sangre de Cristo* (The Procession of the Blood of Christ), which might involve an enactment of the *Crucifixión* (Crucifixion) with a wooden or a human *Cristo*.

There are many exaggerated stories about this climax of the Penitentes' rituals. Generally, there is a detailed reenactment of the march to Calvary, including Christ's three falls, the floggings, the aid of Simon the Cyrenian, Veronica, and so on. If a man is to be crucified then (rather than after a secret procession before dawn on Good Friday), it seems usually to have taken place in front of the *morada* rather than on a remote *Calvario*. Nails may have been used, but there are no eyewitness reports of this. Lee's description is reasonable:

> The time of the crucifixion is an uncertain thing these years, but the method is still the same. The cross that has been dragged many miles is laid with its foot near a small hole. The Christ stands fearless and resolute near it. The men, and sometimes the mother of the victim gather near. The hermano to be crucified as /sic/ laid on the cross, his arms are bound to the shoulder, his legs to the thighs, with ropes. The cross is quickly raised, bearing its human load. The sermon of the seven last words is read. Then all is silent. The Hermano Mayor signals, and the Christ is taken into the morada. The crucifixion varies a little in different localities as does the rest of the proceedings. At times three men are crucified, the two thieves and the Christ. (22, *El Palacio;* p. 10)

The crucifixion is a time of intense emotion. Onlookers kneel, praying and weeping. Death may result from the rites, but this is not as frequent as commonly implied by sensationalized accounts. It is certainly not sought, nor intended.

Las Tinieblas, or "earthquake" ceremonies take place late Good Friday night. These are similar to the Church *Tenebrae* (Latin: darkness, lower world, death) — services commemorating the flight of the apostles and the death of Christ, when darkness descended, rocks split, the earth shook, the dead rose, and the Temple veil was torn. All these ideas are incorporated in the Penitente ritual, which has been mistakenly translated "earthquake" rather than "darkness." In any case, the *Tinieblas* is often open to the public and well attended by villagers (and others) of all ages.

One white candle and twelve yellow ones represent Christ and His disciples. All windows in the *morada* or church are covered, and the door is shut fast throughout the service. A hymn precedes the reading of twelve psalms. One candle is extinguished after each. The *Rezador* hides the white candle, and utter pandemonium breaks loose. Noise from all sources — *pito, matracas* (clackers), drums, chains, pots, clapping, stamping, screaming, etc. — represents the earthquake following Christ's death. In the back or in another room, the penitent Brothers whip themselves for the last time. Periods of cacophony are followed by several minutes of *sudarios* for the dead, whose names are called out by the congregation. The alternation continues for about an hour, after which the white candle is brought forth, the others relighted, and an *alabado* sung. The villagers return home, but the Brothers remain for the *elección* (election) and other business.

Lent ends officially at noon on *Sábado de Gloria* (Saturday of Glory). On Saturday night, it was customary to attend an exuberant *baile* (dance) to celebrate the end of Lenten privations. Good Friday was the climax of the Penitente Holy Week, so *Pascua* (Easter Sunday) services of solemn high mass, processions, and Hallelujahs were somehow anti-climactic, and their observance largely left to official Church supervision.

Persons peripherally cognizant of or blinded to the Brotherhood's organization and traditions have accused the Penitentes of literalism, fanaticism, sadism, and worse. They are unaware of the Spanish religious tradition of deep faith in and mystical devotion to the ideal of a suffering, human Jesus, rather than a triumphant Christ. The Penitentes' imitation was not the slavish replication of Biblical details, but a religious experience. Their worship demanded realistic, immediate participation, expressing their belief that salvation for the soul could not be attained without intense mortification of the body.

INTERPRETIVE ASPECTS

Problems of interpretation can barely be broached in an essay of this length. However, certain weaknesses in the various explanations offered should be clarified. If even elementary distinctions were borne in mind, many injurious misconceptions could be avoided, and perhaps some more appreciative understanding would develop. Thus, while the following treatment is necessarily cursory, the questions raised are important for the critical assessment of sources, as well as for a proper introductory picture of this folk religion.

There are numerous published and unpublished accounts of the Penitentes. The sheer volume is in itself quite telling:

> After having described the 'terrible spectacle' of the Crucifixion, Edith Lane says that 'one feels the sight can no longer be endured, yet is fascinated.' This fascination seems to be an Anglo characteristic. The Pueblo Indians who lived near these Spanish-American communities managed to reject these penances without feeling the same fascination as the Anglos. At least eyewitness accounts do not tell of Indians rubbing elbows with Anglos in the underbrush along the Via Crucis. (15; pp. 42-43)

While these deeper ambivalences and their projections can only be suggested, more blatant biases and analytical shortcomings must be taken into account. Sources have too often been uncritically assembled.

Descriptive materials about the Penitentes are found in many types of writing. These contain eyewitness accounts, secondary and secondhand information, hearsay, and sheer fantasy. Reliability is difficult to establish without comparing sources and checking independent biographical and historical evidence. Early prejudices and ulterior motives are generally easy to identify. Besides journal accounts by traders, travelers, and government officials, there are vehement denunciations by evangelical Protestant missionaries and established Catholics. Lummis' success stimulated a long line of "travel books" and articles on "quaint" customs intended to popularize the Southwest. The turn-of-the-century also marked the beginning of the still-interminable "rehashes" of earlier accounts. These generally obscure descriptions of actual Penitente rituals as witnessed, and certainly contribute to the perpetuation of various misconceptions about the Brotherhood. Nonetheless, good studies do appear, and one of the most accurate and sympathetic descriptions available is in Henderson's *Brothers of Light* (16). With critical caution, then, descriptive bias may be allowed for; it is usually harder to extricate certain interpretive and analytical elements.

In the first place, there is an important historical dimension. When

Anglos began to move into the region after 1821, they reported rituals of a *nonsecret* religion practiced by much of the population. When the relative homogeneity of tradition was disturbed and Hispanic isolation broken, these religious expressions were challenged by uncomprehending Catholic Church officials, by Protestant missionaries, and by English-speaking immigrants with dissimilar value systems as well as different religious persuasions. The Brotherhood gradually became a *secret* sodality to protect traditional culture and faith. Both World Wars and the Depression deeply affected life in rural areas, and membership became more confined to the poorer classes. Although still deeply religious, the Brothers formed a sort of "lobby" or "club," a voluntary association among other groups and allegiances in the more heterogeneous structurings of village life. After 1947, a systematic network of chapters became an official part of organized religion. During each of these periods, the Brotherhoods had different characteristics and social effects, as well as variable psychological consequences for individual members. Descriptions and analyses frequently fail to take such distinctions into account.

Diversity in geographical and social environments must also be considered. For example, the Penitentes have always been strongest in the mountainous regions of north-central New Mexico and southern Colorado. The struggle to survive in these hostile surroundings evolved social structures with variant patterns of property, inheritance, marriage, kinship, and value systems. Communities east, south, and west of this area tended to be more *patrón*-dominated. ("A patron among the Spanish-Americans was and is a prominent individual from a wealthy and powerful family who is able to provide employment, economic security, leadership, decision making, and problem solving for those dependent upon him. His position as patron was based not upon his personal characteristics but upon his ability to perform the institutionalized role of a patron." 21; p. 461) Fraternal relations tended to be more dominant in some Penitente areas (30), with village-wide social responsibility shouldered by seniors within broad generational groupings. Too often, homogeneity throughout New Mexican Hispanic culture has been assumed, and explanations for the Penitentes synthesized by blindly fitting social structure to religious system.

Such psychologizing and sociologizing is pointless because it ignores ecological, sociological, and historical uniquenesses, and because it is usually based on the most tenuous theoretical grounds for relating religious structure and behavior with other cultural aspects. While, e.g., it is undoubtedly true that the idea of what constituted a sin demanding repentance varied to some extent with current social sanctions informally controlled by gossip networks, it is not necessarily also true that all communities operated with identical sanctions or similar networks. Swadesh finds that *vergüenza* (shame, modesty, pride) was less important as an ideal for deportment then "respect and honor" — "a concept which characterizes the quality of relations between people rather than expressing their concern for reputation, the focal point of verguenza" (30; p. 259). To a certain extent, this reflects geographical and historical differences. In other words, studies of Hispanic communities, culture, and personality cannot be accepted as enduring, region-wide ideals, but must be differentiated according to the time, place, and population studied. Comparison must also be made between studies of Penitente and non-Penitente communities. Otherwise, explanatory generalizations relating composite picture to composite picture are fruitless and even defamatory to the people involved.

An important reason for inadequate explanations of the Penitentes is the fact that almost no studies focusing on religion itself have been undertaken in village communities. Religion is treated as only one part of the ethnography, subordinated to description and interpretation of other cultural processes. Consequently, the actual relations which obtain between social structure, social change, economy, education, leisure, communication, etc., and religion (in all its official and unofficial forms) are largely matters of speculation. However, certain functions are generally served by the Brotherhood. Functions on a *cultural* level have already been suggested by stressing the Brotherhood's maintenance of Spanish language and traditions. Other functions are both *psychological,* satisfying individual desires, and *sociological,* satisfying the requirements of the collective unit.

There is general agreement that the Penitentes served important sociological functions, which have already been discussed. A recent report by Knowlton is instructive:

> The diminishing strength of the Penitente Order has had its effect upon village social integration. The yearly calendar of religious

ceremonies no longer involves most of the male population, and village social life has become more monotonous and drab. The Elder Brother of the Penitente lodge cannot maintain control of the behavior of those who violate village mores. No other mechanism has yet developed in the villages to fulfill the social or the religious functions of 'Los Hermanos Penitentes.' Village life, as a result, is marked by vandalism, factionalism, and conflicts between families and individuals. (21; p. 471)

Other studies about the Brotherhood's effect on social change may yet show whether *moradas* were actually an entirely conservative social force.

Psychologically, the Brotherhood assured members social status *and* religious merit. Initiation was a rite of passage into manhood. Membership insured local prestige or at least some sort of social recognition. Participation in the Penitente religious observances helped assuage personal guilt and allowed the expression and satisfaction of deep religious feelings:

. . . they believe in a God who is merciful, but who also, through a very real Purgatory and Hell, can be merciless unless propitiated. Propitiation may be by prayer or 'active' penance, with 'active' penance the more efficacious . . . To the Penitente the symbolic sharing of suffering with Jesus brings him closer to God. Thus the pain and suffering of the flagellant serve a very real psychological purpose and meet what is for him an important felt need. (Hernandez, in 15; p. 378)

Many writers, notably Mills and Grove (26), have found that oversimplified notions of Spanish-American culture prevent more elaborate sociopsychological analyses. Mills leaves the following questions unanswered in his discussion of Penitente art:

Is it guilt, sado-masochism, a nativistic movement, mystical ecstasy, or some combination of these which encouraged wholesale representation of suffering? What aspect of the culture produced a need to suffer so urgent that it spilled over from a realistic re-enactment of Christ's passion into the most powerful folk art to be found within the borders of the United States? What exactly is the relationship between the Spanish-American conception of male authority and male penance? (25; p. 60)

In a real sense, such questions are always unanswerable, certainly in the terms generally proposed.

More impressionistic interpretations have also been presented. One of the most commendable results of these has been to focus attention on "irreducible" religious experiences and needs. Emphasis on worship and religious symbolism has led to a better appreciation of the expressive aspects of Penitentism. Acknowledgement of the meaning and wholeness experienced in any truly religious participation has stimulated a more tolerant attitude toward "strange" and "concrete" religious expressions. Good interpretive accounts of this sort are found in nonfiction works as well as in the fine arts (e.g., 6, 18, 31, 32). Although not consistently factual, they are heuristic and enlightening, excellent antidotes both to unbridled speculation and reductionistic analysis. However, impressionistic accounts cannot substitute for the most important interpretive perspective of all — that of the Brothers themselves, and other Hispanic-Americans within the evolving culture.

Very little has been done to illuminate what might best be termed the "ethnoperspective" of the Penitentes. Limited resources are available in the art, music, rituals, and anecdotes of the Brothers themselves. Some Hispanos outside the Brotherhood have described its activities (e.g., 20, 23), but few Penitentes have explained themselves and their concept of brotherly love and religious devotion. Until they do, neither their ideals nor the actualities of their daily and religious life can be fully understood, and one must remain content with the limited insights afforded by the collected artifacts and expressive verbal lore.

EXPRESSIVE AND MATERIAL CULTURE

In a vast, majestic and inhospitable land, the Penitentes preserved, remolded, and created the effective symbols and instruments of their faith. Their cultural expressions came into being as new patterns of living evolved; they were not simply the degenerate fragments of a dimly-recalled "high" tradition. "Far from being a darkened and enfeebled manifestation of the peripheries, this is an original, positive, and vital culture" (25; pp. 56-57).

A great deal of work has gone into preserving and studying many of these artifacts. Much of it involves technical description and classification, but interpretive studies have appeared, and many are now in progress. The verbal arts have been somewhat neglected, but the Penitentes' folk art and music have been considered, especially the former (e.g., 1, 5, 25, 29). Because good sources exist, the following are only rudimentary remarks about these important aspects.

The Ritual Setting. Usually, each village had at least a church (a *parroquia* — parish church, or a *visita* if no priest were in residence); a *morada;* a *campo santo* in the churchyard, the *morada* yard, or an enclosure by itself; and several nearby or distant sites marked by large crosses and serving as *Calvarios* or destinations for processions. Chávez claims that "a *morada* is a dwelling place or lodge, from the verb *morar* [to dwell, lodge, reside], and not from the feminine of the adjective 'purple,' as some writers have guessed" (8; p. 122). Although *morada* architecture was not uniform, it tended to resemble typical domestic rather than ecclesiastic design. Structures were of stone or *adobe* (sun-dried bricks of mud and straw). They were sometimes adorned with crosses or a bell tower, but were generally constructed to be as inconspicuous as possible. After suffering harassment and pillage, the Brothers kept the few windows boarded up and the doors locked.

Inside, the *morada* usually had at least two rooms — an *oratorio* (chapel) and a meeting room for the Brothers. There was frequently a loft or storage room besides. Furnishings were sparse. Tales of black-draped altars decorated with skulls are common in early accounts. However, most 20th-century reports and photos (e.g., 1, 29, photo p. 41) suggest that the atmosphere is one of simplicity and humble domesticity rather than dark mystery.

Ritual Paraphernalia. Besides the sacred images, Penitentes required little ritual equipment. *Disciplinas* (whips) were usually about two feet long, made of braided yucca fibers or rope, and dipped in water or an antiseptic solution to make them heavier. The *Sangrador* cut the *obligación* with *pedernales* (flints) — sharp stones or pieces of glass. (The gashes, which did not affect the musculature, assured a free flow of blood so scourgings would not cause welts and bruises.) A tub for washing the penitents' wounds was kept in the meeting or storage room. Timbers for the *maderos* were cut when the sap began to rise, so the bark could be stripped off more easily. These huge penitential crosses were often left outside the *morada* through all weather. Wooden *candelabros* (candelabra) —

some painted black *(tenebrarios)* and used in Lenten services, lanterns (candle and kerosene), *matracas* (raucous wooden clackers), drums, and other noise-making devices complete the basic inventory.

Santos (Sacred images).   Paintings, statues, prints, and other graphic representations, as well as holy persons or objects, are included in this generic term. *Retablos* (two-dimensional images) and *bultos* (figures in the round) were carved by *santeros* (*santo*-makers; also, custodians of holy images). Stimulated by the need for objects of religious devotion in Spanish colonial days, an intense folk art developed, flowered, and faded in less than 150 years. "Now, when the deep sense of devotion has deserted the craftsman, we can look back and trace the entire development of the New Mexico *santero* school from its isolated beginnings in the second half of the eighteenth century through its classic prime up to 1860 and its decline in the face of foreign ridicule and commercial substitutes, to 1907" (5; p. 23).

Santos were integral to daily religious devotions and calendric ritual observances. They were not mere objects of contemplation but intimate participants in Hispanic Life:

MORADA INTERIOR. Photographed by Dorothy Stewart, 1940. From the Collections in the Museum of New Mexico, photo no. 30439. By courtesy of the Museum of New Mexico, Santa Fe.

> Each saint had his special job to do and, in doing it, was treated
> like a member of the family . . . A 'santo' that did not do its job
> might be turned to the wall or locked in a trunk . . . The natural
> order itself has been conceived as integral with a family scheme,
> and so those tasks which go beyond rational technology are accom-
> plished by daily processes of human interaction, reward, punish-
> ment, and persuasion. (25; p. 59)

Santos were no less important in Penitente observances. Realistic,
sanguinary figures of Christ, some nearly life size, represented *Jesús
Nazareno* (*Ecce Homo,* or Man of Sorrows), *Cristo Crucificado* (Christ
Crucified), and *El Santo Entierro* (Christ in the Holy Sepulcher).
Since the limbs were articulated, the same figure could be used for all
aspects of the Passion, although some *moradas* owned different *bultos*
for each. Images of *Nuestra Señora de la Soledad* (Our Lady of Soli-
tude), *Nuestra Señora de los Dolores* (Our Lady of Sorrows), *San
Juan Nepomuceno* (St. John of Nepomuk — a Bohemian priest mar-
tyred for keeping confidences; a symbol of secrecy), and others, were
popular. There were also any number of smaller crucifixes and religious images in the *morada.* Often, in fact, *santos* no longer tolerated
in the local church would be preserved by the Brothers.

La Muerte (Death) was a part of most rituals into the early 20th
century. Also called *Doña Sebastiana,* this carved skeleton carried a
hatchet or bow and arrow (believed once to have struck and killed a
faithless bystander) and rode in a miniature of the New Mexican ox-
cart. Stones were added to intensify the penance of dragging the
carreta de la muerte (death cart) — a literal enactment of man's
struggle against death. The death cart at Las Trampas was kept in the
church itself, to the right of the main door. According to Leyba,
"they believed that if any person would pray to the image of
Sebastiana, that their lives would be prolonged, so each time they
came to the church, a prayer was offered to this image, and again and
again they prayed with devotion before it" (23; p. 49). Such images
were and sometimes still are part of Spanish and Mexican Holy Week
rites, but they came to play a uniquely realistic role in New Mexican
Penitente observances.

Alabados (Religious hymns).   All Penitente ritual is extremely ortho-
dox, so it is not surprising that many
of their hymns, litanies, and *oraciones* (prayers) are traditional. An

alabado (from the opening words: *alabado sea,* praised be) is a hymn in praise of the Sacraments, and can be found in variant forms throughout the Spanish-speaking world. In New Mexico, it has come to refer to any religious hymn sung during ritual observances, at wakes for the dead or the saints, and for family worship. Versions already collected have been traced to Spain, some as far back as the 15th century; to Mexico; and to local poets.

Many Penitente *alabados* honored the Passion of Our Lord or exhorted the sinner to repent, but there were also songs in praise of the Virgin, the saints, the dead, and even some appropriate to the hour of dawn. Because they were quite long, hymns were transcribed into private *cuadernos* (copybooks) for safekeeping. They were sung without accompaniment (except, sometimes, the *pito*) by a *cantador* or recognized village singer. During Penitente observances, the Brothers would join in singing the chorus.

Rael (27), as yet the only detailed study available, classifies most *alabados* into the predominate form of Spanish folk poetry — the eight-syllable verse quatrain with second and fourth lines assonant or rhymed. The following example is from the W.P.A. Files at the History Library of the Museum of New Mexico, Santa Fe. The text, sung during the rite of crucifixion, was copied by L. Brown from a *cuaderno* loaned by a Penitente in Rio Arriba County, New Mexico. The first and last stanzas and Brown's translation (File No. 5, Drawer No. 5, Folder No. 5, No. 67) read:

Oh Jesús, por mis delitos	Oh Jesus, for my faults
Padeciste tal dolor:	you suffered so much pain;
A tus pies arrepentido	At your feet you see me
Me ves, dulce Redentor.	repentant, Sweet Redeemer.
A Jesús en Cruz clavado	Look, Oh sinner, on the Christ,
Contemplale, oh pecador;	Jesus nailed to the Cross;
Ve al hijo del Eterno	Look on the Son of the Eternal
Expirando por tu amor.	Expiring for love of you.

The music for such hymns seems to contain elements of old Church modes, with perhaps some Moorish influence. Regionally, the style was known as the "Penitente" or *"alabado"* manner of singing. Melodies were also recognized by local variations and referred to as the version from a particular village.

Verbal Lore. In the W.P.A. Files and throughout the published literature, there are scattered reports of beliefs, sayings, anecdotes, and legends involving the Penitentes. These range from the name of a particularly heavy *madero* through the stratagems used by Penitentes to explain their Holy Week absences to a number of tales about the mysterious appearance of ghostly flagellants (e.g., 15; pp. 382-383). Like the *alabado* texts, they have not been systematically examined for new insights into the Brotherhood's beliefs and attitudes. Until such a study is made, the following item, which has often been recorded in the region, is illustrative:

Penitente pecador,	Penitente sinner,
Porque te andas azotando?	Why do you go whipping yourself?
Por una vaca que robé	'For a cow that I stole,
Y aqui la ando disquitando.	And here I go paying for her.' (24;p.108)

Although this has been cynically cited by many unsympathetic outsiders ("Whip today; sin tomorrow."), it is also part of the folklore among the region's Hispanic peoples. It might be that such a stanza, used by non-Penitente neighbors or perhaps by some Brothers themselves, indicates an amused acceptance of the irony of man's frailty despite his best efforts for perfection.

These tangible forms can be the source of many fruitful insights. Ultimately, however, the Brothers themselves must say which forms are good and which bad, which beautiful and which ugly, which appropriate and which inappropriate. For the art, the music, and the rhetoric are in large part expressions of their religious experience.

CONCLUSION

Los Hermanos Penitentes, then, are not as mysterious, as sensational, as subversive, or even as stereotyped as commonly thought. They are religious men, but they are also individuals living within the world, where they struggle to retain at least something of their Hispanic heritage amid poverty and Anglo pressure. Too often, others have spoken for these Brothers. Today, their own descriptions of religious experience and their ideas about good neighbors and good brothers are much needed.

SELECTED BIBLIOGRAPHY

An exhaustive bibliography of some six hundred annotated entries has been assembled for publication in a longer study of the Penitentes. Until this monograph is published, the following items should be among the most useful available to anyone with a further interest in the Brotherhood.

1. Ahlborn, Richard E. *The Penitente Moradas of Abiquiú.* Contributions from the Museum of History and Technology, Paper 63. Washington, D.C.: Smithsonian Institution Press, 1968.
2. Austin, Mary. "The Trail of the Blood: An Account of the Penitent Brotherhood of New Mexico," *Century Magazine,* n.s., 86 (1924), 35-44. (Also published in *The Land of Journey's Ending,* George Allen & Unwin, London, 1924, pp. 347-372.)
3. Barker, S. Omar. "Los Penitentes," *Overland Monthly and Out West Magazine,* 82 (April, 1924), 151-153, 179-180.
4. Beshoar, Barron B. "Western Trails to Calvary," in *The 1949 Brand Book,* ed. Don Bloch. Denver, Colorado: The Westerners, Denver Posse, 1950, pp. 119-148.
5. Boyd, E. "The New Mexico Santero," *El Palacio,* 76 (1969), 1-24. (Also published separately by the Museum of New Mexico Press, Santa Fe, 1969, as an exhibition catalogue.)
6. Bright, Robert. *The Life and Death of Little Jo.* Garden City, New York: Doubleday, Doran, 1944. (Novel.)
7. Burma, John H. "Los Hermanos Penitentes: A Case Study of the Cultural Survival of Flagellation," in *Spanish-Speaking Groups in the United States.* Durham, North Carolina: Duke University Press, 1954, pp. 188-198.
8. Chávez, Fray Angélico. "The Penitentes of New Mexico," *New Mexico Historical Review,* 29 (1954), 97-123.
9. Darley, Alex. M. *The Passionists of the Southwest, or The Holy Brotherhood: A Revelation of the 'Penitentes'.* Pueblo, Colorado: n.n., 1893. (Reprinted by Rio Grande Press, Glorieta, New Mexico, 1968.)
10. Edmonson, Munro S. *Los Manitos: A Study of Institutional Values.* New Orleans, Louisiana: Middle American Research Institute, Tulane University, 1957. (Reprint from Middle American Research Institute, Pub. 25, pp. 1-72.)
11. Fisher, Reginald. "Notes on the Relation of the Franciscans to the Penitentes," *El Palacio,* 48 (1941), 263-271.
12. Foster, George M. " 'Cofradía' and 'Compadrazgo' in Spain and Spanish America," *Southwestern Journal of Anthropology,* 9 (1953), 1-28.
13. _____.*Culture and Conquest: America's Spanish Heritage.* Viking Fund Publications in Anthropology, No. 27. Chicago: Quadrangle Books, 1960.
14. González, Nancie L. *The Spanish-Americans of New Mexico: A Heritage of Pride.* Albuquerque: University of New Mexico Press, 1969.
15. Greenway, John (ed.). *Folklore of the Great West: Selections from Eighty-three Years of the 'Journal of American Folklore'.* Palo Alto, California: American West Publishing, 1969. (Especially pp. 365-383.)
16. Henderson, Alice Corbin. *Brothers of Light: The Penitentes of the Southwest,* illus. William Penhallow Henderson. New York: Harcourt, Brace, 1937. (Reprinted by Rio Grande Press, Chicago, 1962.)

46

17. Holmes, Jack E. *Politics in New Mexico.* Albuquerque: University of New Mexico Press, 1967. (Especially pp. 33-49.)
18. Horgan, Paul. "Mortality," in *Great River: The Rio Grande in North American History.* New York: Rinehart, 1954, vol. I, pp. 374-382.
19. Horka-Follick, Lorayne Ann. *Los Hermanos Penitentes: A Vestige of Medievalism in Southwestern United States.* Great West and Indian Series, No. 38. Los Angeles: Westernlore Press, 1969.
20. Jaramillo, Cleo(fas M.). *Romance of a Little Village Girl.* San Antonio, Texas: Naylor, 1955.
21. Knowlton, Clark S. "Changing Spanish-American Villages of Northern New Mexico," *Sociology and Social Research,* 53 (1969), 455-474.
22. Lee, Laurence F. *Los Hermanos Penitentes.* Unpublished B.A. thesis in English, University of New Mexico, 1910. (Most of this was published anonymously in *El Palacio,* vol. 8, January 31, 1920, pp. 2-20.)
23. Leyba, Ely. "The Church of the Twelve Apostles," *New Mexico Magazine,* 11 (June, 1933), 19-21, 47-52.
24. Lummis, Charles F. "The Penitent Brothers," in *The Land of Poco Tiempo.* Albuquerque: University of New Mexico Press, illustrated facsimile ed., 1966, pp. 77-108. (First published 1893.)
25. Mills, George. *The People of the Saints.* Colorado Springs: The Taylor Museum of The Colorado Springs Fine Arts Center, n.d. (c. 1967.)
26. _____,and Richard Grove. *Lucifer and the Crucifer: The Enigma of the Penitentes.* Colorado Springs: The Taylor Museum of The Colorado Springs Fine Arts Center, 1966. (Reprinted from *The 1955 Brand Book* of the Denver Posse of the Westerners, ed. Alan Swallow, 1956, pp. 252-292.)
27. Rael, Juan B. *The New Mexican 'Alabado':* With Transcription of Music by Eleanor Hague. Stanford University Publications, University Series, Language and Literature, vol. 9, no. 3. Stanford, California: Stanford University Press, 1951.
28. Schwartz, Kessel, and James Chaplin. *Los Hermanos Penitentes. Scripta Humanistica Kentuckiensia,* II. Lexington: University of Kentucky Library, 1958.
29. Shalkop, Robert L. *Arroyo Hondo: The Folk Art of a New Mexican Village.* Colorado Springs: The Taylor Museum of The Colorado Springs Fine Arts Center, 1969.
30. Swadesh, Frances Leon. *Hispanic Americans of the Ute Frontier from the Chama Valley to the San Juan Basin 1694-1960.* Unpublished Ph.D. dissertation, University of Colorado, 1966. (Also available as Research Report No. 50, Tri-Ethnic Research Project, University of Colorado, Boulder, 1966.)
31. Udell, Isaac L. "In The Dust of The Valley," *South Dakota Review,* 7 (1969), 9-105.
32. _____. *The Penitentes.* Denver, Colorado: The Cosmopolitan Art Gallery, n.d.
33. Wallrich, William. "Auxiliadoras de la Morada," *Southwestern Lore,* 16 (1950), 4-10.
34. Woodward, Dorothy. *The Penitentes of New Mexico.* Unpublished Ph.D. dissertation, Yale University, 1935.